W9-ACR-560

Let us give honor to whom honor is due; to those who conceived this mighty project and to those who made its building possible; to the engineers who designed it and the directors and management that built it. Let us pay tribute to the men whose hands actually constructed it.

—San Francisco Mayor Angelo J. Rossi, 1937

BUILDING THE GOLDEN GATE BRIDGE

COURAGE · INGENUITY · VISION

GOLDEN GATE NATIONAL PARKS CONSERVANCY
GOLDEN GATE BRIDGE, HIGHWAY AND TRANSPORTATION DISTRICT
SAN FRANCISCO, CALIFORNIA

INTRODUCTION

Great bridges define great cities. Built for the most practical of reasons, a purely functional bridge is an unremarkable connection across a gap in the landscape. When engineers and architects go further; when they have the imagination and will to defy accepted wisdom and design a heart-stoppingly beautiful span across a treacherous and picturesque strait; when science, art, and resolve are manifested—then, on those rare occasions, a masterpiece is created, as it was in America in the 1930s: the iconic Golden Gate Bridge.

> **I looked up and there were the black steel of the travelers and the red steel of the towers and hoses running in all directions, and I just was amazed at all the activity.**
>
> —*Fred Divita, Bridgeworker*

Bridge construction began on January 5, 1933, but the road to that day was a long one. Formal efforts began in 1919, when San Francisco City Engineer Michael M. O'Shaughnessy began to evaluate the possibility of bridging the Golden Gate Strait. Among the people O'Shaughnessy talked to was Chicago-based engineer Joseph B. Strauss, who proved to be enthusiastic about the project and willing to take it on. Then, in 1923, Sonoma County banker Franklin P. Doyle convened a meeting in Santa Rosa of representatives from all northern California counties. From that meeting emerged the Bridging the Golden Gate Association.

Their first challenge was to convince the state legislature to create a special district to plan, design, and oversee construction of the bridge. They succeeded, and the Golden Gate Bridge and Highway District was formed later that year. Then, each northern California county was asked to either opt into or out of the district. By 1928, six of the twenty-one counties (San Francisco, Marin, Sonoma, Napa, Mendocino, and Del Norte) had joined the district and committed to moving the ambitious project forward.

> **On some days, you were working up on top—working above the fog—and it really looked like a blanket of snow up there. It's unbelievable how pretty it was up above the fog.**
>
> —*Fred Brusati, Electrician*

This was much more than a specialized agenda pursued by a small group of influential people. In November 1930, during a time in which no federal funds were available, residents of the six counties went to the polls and voted to back bridge construction bonds with their homes, their vineyards, their businesses, their very livelihoods. They took an almost unimaginable risk, essentially betting everything they had during a time of deep economic gloom to ensure that the bridge would be built.

Matching their conviction, local San Franciscan A. P. Giannini—the Italian immigrant who had founded what became the Bank of America in 1904 as an institution for the "little fellow"—put the resources of his bank on the line. Over a period of time, Bank of America purchased the $35 million in bonds that helped the drive for the new bridge clear its final financial hurdle.

A decade after the Bridging the Golden Gate Association came into being—a time during which people from all walks of life remained unswerving in their belief that it was both possible and vitally important to span the strait—the dangerous and daunting task of translating designs on paper to steel and concrete began. The strait's currents, fog, and wind further heightened the engineering challenges.

Far from the offices, boardrooms, and courtrooms in which the bridge had been discussed, developed, and argued, ironworkers, roustabouts, and construction workers from the district put their backs into the job. And the Golden Gate Bridge rose—anchorages, pylons, towers, cables, roadway, approaches, all in logical progression.

Everybody who worked on that bridge knew it was special. I'm sure that any man who had anything to do with the bridge thought of it as his bridge.

—*Slim Lambert, Roustabout*

Perhaps because of its location, or the exceptional engineering feat it represented, its story was extensively documented. This collection of construction-progress photos, taken by photographers Charles M. Hiller and Bev Washburn, is from the holdings of the Golden Gate Bridge, Highway and

Transportation District. From the "unbridged" Golden Gate Strait to the bridge's opening to traffic on May 28, 1937, each photo tells a vital part of the story.

When you look at these photographs, consider where the photographers must have been in order to take them. Many were shot from an airplane, and for others, the photographer would have had to scramble along construction footbridges or crouch in the shadow of massive machinery, all while carrying a heavy camera or two, lenses, extra film, and perhaps a tripod. After the bridge was completed, Washburn mounted the photographs in oversize albums, two of which are held by the Golden Gate Bridge, Highway and Transportation District.

This was, after all, the bridge that many said couldn't be built. Thanks to Washburn and Hiller, we can follow the progress of this engineering marvel from anchorage excavation and the literal high-wire act of cable-spinning through paving of the roadway and painting of the steel. An astounding effort, an astounding bridge.

BUILDING THE GOLDEN GATE BRIDGE

Golden Gate Strait, circa 1932: Fort Point (right) and the Lime Point lighthouse and fog signal station (left) face one another across the strait.

Circa 1932
Pre-construction view from the San Francisco shoreline
near Fort Point.

FEBRUARY 1933

Construction commenced on January 5, 1933, and in
the days that followed, contractors began assembling
materials and equipment at the Fort Point staging area.

FEBRUARY 1933
Pacific Bridge Company was the primary contractor
for construction of the tower piers and the
San Francisco (south) tower fender.

FEBRUARY 1933

Unlike the Marin (north) tower, the San Francisco tower fender and pier had to be constructed in the turbulent, fast-moving waters of the Golden Gate Strait. To reach the work site, a 1,100-foot-long access trestle was built from the shoreline near Fort Point.

AUGUST 1933

Before construction of the San Francisco tower fender and pier could begin, the surface of the bedrock, 110 feet below the water, had to be leveled. Dynamite-filled bombs loosened the rock, and debris was removed with a Whirley derrick. The man in the foreground is Earle C. Anthony, a prominent San Francisco car dealer and radio station owner.

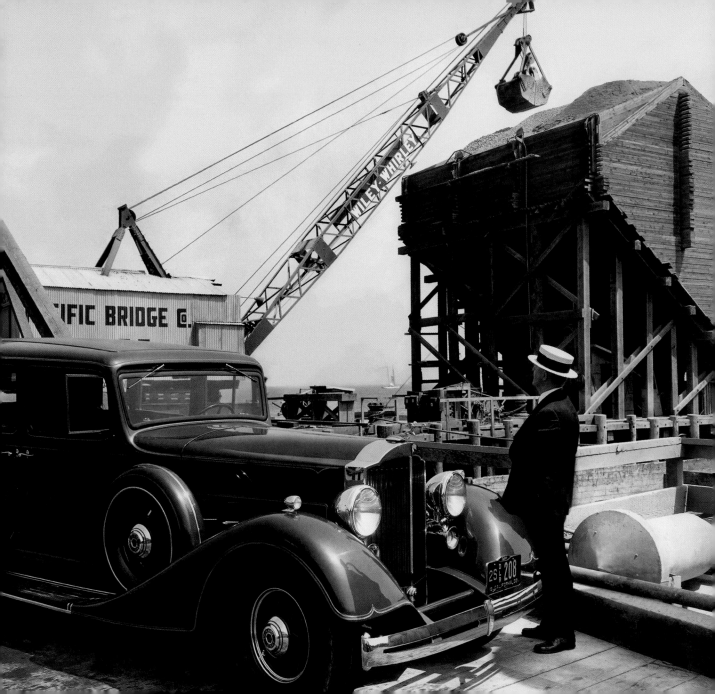

AUGUST 1933

On August 14, just two days after this photo was taken, the outbound *Sidney M. Hauptman*, a McCormick Line steamship, crashed into the newly completed access trestle in thick fog, causing additional costs and delays while repairs were made.

AUGUST 1933

The bridge project required enormous amounts of
concrete. To supply it quickly and efficiently, batching
plants were set up on both the Marin and San Francisco
sides. The concrete was mixed on-site and delivered
where needed by a fleet of Golden Gate Atlas Materials
Company trucks.

AUGUST 1933
Barges delivered Portland cement and a mixture of
sand and gravel to the batching plants, where the
materials were stored in silos and bins. Once the
ingredients were combined, water was added and the
concrete was transferred to trucks and taken to the
work site.

AUGUST 1933

Inside one of the batching plants, visitors test out the mixing bin mechanism; the large scale behind them was used to measure the dry ingredients and ensure consistency.

AUGUST 1933
The Marin and San Francisco anchorages and pylons
were built by Barrett & Hilp. Here, excavation for the
San Francisco anchorage is underway.

AUGUST 1933
A new seawall under construction on the San Francisco shoreline.

SEPTEMBER 1933

Bridge construction required extensive excavation and reconfiguration of the land near Fort Point. On many levels, construction of the Golden Gate Bridge changed this landscape forever.

SEPTEMBER 1933
This aerial shot provides a good view of the interior
of Fort Point as well as ongoing construction of the
San Francisco anchorage.

SEPTEMBER 1933

Repairs to the access trestle, which had been damaged in August, are complete. The trestle would be battered once again in December during a two-day gale, sustaining 800 feet of wreckage. Shortly thereafter, a new round of repairs began, and were completed on March 8, 1934.

SEPTEMBER 1933
The Marin tower pier, completed in June 1933 and
ready for tower construction. Unlike the San Francisco
tower, it was built on land only 20 feet underwater.

SEPTEMBER 1933

The hillside above the Marin tower pier, ready for
construction of the north anchorage and pylons; work
on the Marin tower would begin in November.

DECEMBER 1933
Construction of the Marin tower, which began on
November 7, is well underway. The concrete batching
plant and Fort Baker can be seen in the background.

DECEMBER 1933

Steel sections are lifted into place with a traveling
derrick system.

FEBRUARY 1934

Marin tower in progress; the tower legs are connected
and stabilized with X-bracing. Later, the braced sections
visible above the roadway will be concealed by Art
Deco–style fluted steel.

FEBRUARY 1934

On the San Francisco side, progress is made on the first of two pylons that will house and frame the Fort Point arch.

APRIL 1934

A bird's-eye view, with Fort Winfield Scott in the foreground. Fort Scott, a sub-post of the Presidio, was established as the headquarters of the Artillery District of San Francisco in 1912.

JUNE 1934

The Marin tower, topped off in May, awaits construction
of the cable saddles.

JUNE 1934

At a year and a half into construction, great progress has been made: the Marin tower is ready for its cable saddles, the first of two pylons on the San Francisco side nears completion to the north of Fort Point, and construction of the San Francisco tower fender is underway.

JUNE 1934

The San Francisco tower fender construction site (lower right). This was the first time in bridge-building history that a structure of such gigantic proportions would be built in the open sea.

SEPTEMBER 1934
Appearing to be tethered to the shoreline by the trestle,
the San Francisco tower fender nears completion.
Made up of twenty-two sections, it was constructed in
horizontal layers, much like a brick wall.

SEPTEMBER 1934
Dubbed a "giant bathtub" by the workers, the San
Francisco tower fender was built to protect the tower
pier from damage by stray ships and intense currents.

NOVEMBER 1934
San Franciscans had a front-row seat as the bridge
began to take shape.

NOVEMBER 1934
The fender prior to dewatering, which took place on
November 27, 1934.

DECEMBER 1934
Pacific Bridge Company's Whirley derrick on a work
platform built atop the fender wall.

DECEMBER 1934

Men standing inside the recently dewatered fender.
Note the six vertical shafts (of eight total). These hollow
shafts, which were 4 feet in diameter and encased in
concrete poured to a height of 65 feet from bedrock
prior to dewatering, led to small inspection chambers
at bedrock level. Accessing the chambers via ladders,
geologists and engineers made their final inspections
to confirm that the bedrock could support the weight of
the bridge.

JANUARY 1935

On January 3, the San Francisco tower pier reached its final height of 44 feet above the water. The surface was then leveled to within 1/32 of an inch using a trolley-mounted grinding wheel.

FEBRUARY 1935

Despite being delayed by damage to the access trestle, work on the San Francisco tower commenced in January and was completed on June 28, just six months later.

MARCH 1935
Chief Engineer Joseph Strauss's vision of a bridge
across the Golden Gate Strait came closer to reality
with each advance in the bridge's construction.

MARCH 1935

As the project nears the half-way point, construction
is well along, and the start of cable spinning is just
around the corner.

MARCH 1935

Closer view of the San Francisco tower going up.

APRIL 1935

The two towers face one another across the Golden
Gate Strait; they will soon be joined by the construction
of footwalks in preparation for main cable spinning.

APRIL 1935

Crissy Army Airfield (top left) provides a backdrop for the steadily progressing bridge. Established in 1919, the airfield had long struggled with a lack of space to expand, as well as the high winds and pockets of deep fog that made for dangerous landings and take-offs. When it became clear that a bridge would be built across the strait, the army initiated plans to relocate the airfield to a less hazardous location. Closed in the summer of 1936, it was used thereafter on an as-needed basis by spotter planes and helicopters.

APRIL 1935
San Francisco-side structures: tower, two pylons, and
anchorage.

JUNE 1935
Concrete pylons, both of which will rise to 243 feet, frame Fort Point. To avoid demolishing the fort, engineers designed a steel arch to span the Civil War–era brick fortification.

AUGUST 1935

The massive concrete pylons eclipse the Fort Point
lighthouse.

SEPTEMBER 1935

A vertigo-inducing view toward the base of the Marin tower from a point near its top. (Note the Art Deco styling of the steel on the tower's horizontal struts.)

SEPTEMBER 1935
The Marin anchorage housing and pylon loom above the
batching plant that provided the concrete used to build
them.

SEPTEMBER 1935

On August 2, a McClintic-Marshall barge brought 5,000
feet of wire rope across the Golden Gate Strait from
the Marin anchorage to the San Francisco anchorage.
Derricked up and over the tops of the towers, it served
as the first of the foundation wires for the footwalks.

SEPTEMBER 1935
Atop the Marin tower, crews construct a work platform
in preparation for main cable spinning.

SEPTEMBER 1935

Cables intended to support the footwalks are strung about three feet below the projected line of the main cables. They assume a catenary curve, a shape created when a cable is supported at both ends and acted upon only by its own weight.

SEPTEMBER 1935

Parallel footwalks are constructed with cables and ten-foot panels of redwood planking.

OCTOBER 1935
With the completion of the footwalks in late September,
the bridge's iconic outline is suggested.

OCTOBER 1935

Some of the complex rigging required for cable spinning
is put into place.

OCTOBER 1935
The footwalks are rigged for cable spinning. Notice
the catwalks (crosswalks) that connect and assist in
stabilizing the parallel walkways.

OCTOBER 1935
Parallel footwalks were connected by catwalks at
quarter spans and midspan; this is the cable-spinning
transfer station under construction at midspan.

OCTOBER 1935

Workers on a catwalk take a moment to watch a ship
passing underneath (and wave to the photographer).

OCTOBER 1935
Cable crews prepare for the next phase of the job.
The main cables were spun by crews from John A.
Roebling's Sons.

DECEMBER 1935
Taken two months after the parallel footwalks were in place, the soon-to-be shape of the bridge can be seen even more clearly in this photo.

JANUARY 1936
Ground-level view down the San Francisco tower access
trestle toward Marin. Pelicans have long been frequent
bridge visitors.

JANUARY 1936

To construct the two main cables, an overhead tramway line was strung from anchorage to anchorage. A cable wire-spinning wheel (pictured here) picked up loops of wire at one anchorage and carried them to the midspan transfer station, where they were shifted to another wheel that carried them on to the opposite end.

JANUARY 1936
View from the south tower; banded cable bundles are
loosely grouped in the center.

JANUARY 1936
After the main cable strands were placed in the
spinning saddle atop the tower, lifting straps are
cut away.

JANUARY 1936
Workers lift completed main cable bundles out of the
spinning saddle.

JANUARY 1936

Cable bundles are secured during spinning of additional
bundles.

JANUARY 1936
Each main cable has sixty-one bundles of galvanized
steel wire; here, cable formers maintain the bundles in
vertical rows as they are spun.

JANUARY 1936

Cable bundles disappear through the opening in the plyon and then into the anchorage.

JUNE 1936
Cable-compacting machines are used to compress
the wire bundles.

JUNE 1936

As the strands are compressed, the main cable is measured to ensure that a consistent diameter is maintained.

JUNE 1936

Main cables complete, the bridge is ready for the vertical suspender ropes and construction of the stiffening truss and roadway.

JUNE 1936
On the San Francisco side, construction of the high
viaduct of the Presidio approach road (later named
Doyle Drive) is underway.

AUGUST 1936
At the northern end, the Marin approach viaduct
structures take shape.

SEPTEMBER 1936

Installed in the summer of 1936, the safety net progresses along the bridge's underbelly just ahead of the stiffening truss. It eventually stretched from one side of the bridge to the other. Considered the most dramatic safety measure in the history of bridge building, it was responsible for saving nineteen lives. These nineteen men dubbed themselves members of the Half-way to Hell Club.

SEPTEMBER 1936

Cable bands were added to the main cable at fifty-foot intervals; the bands protect the main cable and provide a place from which to hang the vertical suspender ropes.

SEPTEMBER 1936
Pairs of vertical suspender ropes will connect the roadway truss to the main cables.

SEPTEMBER 1936

Workers rig the safety net in advance of roadway truss
construction.

OCTOBER 1936
Tightening the cable band bolts.

OCTOBER 1936

To build the suspended structure, steel was loaded
onto barges, towed to the site, unloaded onto platforms
at the tower bases, then lifted to roadway level by
Chicago booms.

OCTOBER 1936

View from beneath the San Francisco tower; both the
safety net, which was ten feet wider than the bridge,
and the evolving roadway truss and floor beam
structure are visible.

OCTOBER 1936
The Presidio approach road (later, Doyle Drive) casts a
shadow over army buildings near Crissy Army Airfield.

OCTOBER 1936

The main-span roadway approaches the center.

NOVEMBER 1936
While roadway construction proceeds, painters coat the
vertical suspender ropes with a protective layer of lead-
based paint tinted International Orange.

NOVEMBER 1936

Roadway steel truss sections are positioned by traveling cranes; workers connect the truss sections to the vertical suspender ropes.

DECEMBER 1936
Work crews place the steel girders of the roadway
stiffening truss.

DECEMBER 1936
Perching awkwardly on narrow steel girders, men work
on the assembly of the roadway stiffening truss.

JANUARY 1937
View of roadway and sidewalk construction from the
San Francisco side.

JANUARY 1937
The roadway is nearly ready for its concrete surface; the
first roadway concrete was poured on January 19, 1937.

JANUARY 1937
Plywood forms are installed between the roadway
stringers as a foundation for reinforcing steel and
concrete.

FEBRUARY 1937
Painting continues; suspended in bosun's chairs,
workers were vulnerable to wind gusts and other
weather-related surprises.

FEBRUARY 1937
Workers spot-weld the reinforcing steel in a section of
roadway before concrete is poured.

MARCH 1937
Concrete was poured in fifty-foot lengths. Expansion
joints were installed between each length to alleviate
strain from contraction and expansion of the roadway
floor system.

APRIL 1937

The Last Rivet Ceremony was held at midspan on April
27 to mark the end of construction. Sonora banker
Charles H. Segerstrom (at right) donated the gold rivet.

THE LAST RIVET
of the
GOLDEN GATE BRIDGE
A rivet of California gold was driven at this spot.
PRESENTED TO THE
GOLDEN GATE BRIDGE and HIGHWAY DISTRICT
by
CHARLES H. SEGERSTROM
APRIL 27, 1937

APRIL 1937
Chief engineer Joseph Strauss (hatless, center)
positions the ceremonial gold last rivet for buckerup
Edward Murphy (right, holding tool) and riveter Ed
"Ironhorse" Stanley (left, with rivet gun) to drive home.

APRIL 1937

A large crowd gathered at the San Francisco end
of the span to watch the Last Rivet Ceremony. But
because there was no forge to heat it, the golden rivet
disintegrated right before everyone's eyes when Stanley
tried to tighten it down.

MAY 1937
Though some of the construction equipment remains
in place atop the towers, the bridge is ready for
"Pedestrian Day" festivities.

MAY 27, 1937

Braving early-morning fog and brisk ocean wind, thousands turned out on Pedestrian Day for a first-hand experience of the new engineering marvel. News reports of the day estimated that 125,000 to as many as 200,000 people participated in this public celebration. Some tried to set records, including: the first to cross on stilts or roller skates; first to walk backward or run across; first to walk the center line; first to cross playing the tuba; and first baby to be rolled across the span in a carriage.

MAY 27, 1937

Taking a break from the excitement, Chief Engineer
Joseph Strauss shared a quiet moment with a pal.

MAY 28, 1937

As part of the opening day celebration, three ceremonial barriers were removed. The first event took place at 10:15 AM at the Marin end of the bridge, where three championship lumberjacks competed in the International California Redwood Log-Barrier Sawing Contest, cutting through the logs and opening the Marin approach.

MAY 28, 1937

At 10:30 AM, the second barrier—three chains made
of precious metals—was removed at the chain-cutting
ceremony, which took place at the Marin tower, marking
the San Francisco-Marin County line. Frank P. Doyle,
Golden Gate Bridge and Highway District board member
and treasurer of the Redwood Empire Association
(right), cuts the copper chain. The gold chain was
parted by Board President William P. Filmer, and San
Francisco Mayor Angelo J. Rossi cut the silver chain.

MAY 28, 1937

At 10:50 AM, the third and final "barrier" was broken at the toll plaza on the San Francisco end of the bridge. In the Floral Gate Ceremony, the Fiesta Queens (left) formed a living gate, which was opened to dignitaries following presentation of the completed bridge to the Golden Gate Bridge and Highway District by Chief Engineer Strauss (center) and acceptance by Board President Filmer.

MAY 28, 1937
At noon, President Franklin D. Roosevelt pressed a
telegraph key in the White House to formally open the
bridge to traffic, and shortly thereafter, cars streamed
south from Marin County into San Francisco for the
first time.

MAY 28, 1937

The dream of Golden Gate Bridge Chief Engineer Joseph
Strauss becomes a reality when the span is opened to
traffic on May 28, 1937. In the first stanza of his poem,
The Mighty Task Is Done, he writes,

"At last the mighty task is done;
Resplendent in the western sun
The Bridge looms mountain high;
Its titan piers grip ocean floor,
Its great steel arms link shore with shore,
Its towers pierce the sky."

Copyright © 2012 Golden Gate National Parks Conservancy and Golden Gate Bridge, Highway and Transportation District

All rights reserved. No part of this book may be reproduced in any form without written permission from the publisher. For information, contact Golden Gate National Parks Conservancy, Bldg. 201 Fort Mason, San Francisco, California 94123, or Golden Gate Bridge, Highway and Transportation District, PO Box 9000 Presidio Sta., San Francisco, California 94129

Published in cooperation with the Golden Gate Bridge, Highway and Transportation District

Angelo J. Rossi quote: *Official Program, Golden Gate Bridge Fiesta, San Francisco, May 27–June 2, 1937.*

Bridge workers' quotes: San Francisco State University/Labor Archives and Research Center, "The Building of the Golden Gate Bridge Project" oral histories (1987); Harvey Schwartz, interviewer.

Photographs: From the holdings of the Golden Gate Bridge, Highway and Transportation District.

ISBN 978-1-932519-20-4
Library of Congress Control Number: 2011943602

Art Direction: Robert Lieber
Design: Vivian Young
Editor: Susan Tasaki
Production: Sarah Lau Levitt
Golden Gate Bridge Advisor: Mary Currie

PARKS FOR ALL FOREVER™

The Golden Gate National Parks Conservancy is the nonprofit membership organization created to preserve the Golden Gate National Parks, enhance the experiences of park visitors, and build a community dedicated to conserving the parks for the future. The Parks Conservancy partners with the National Park Service, Presidio Trust, and Golden Gate Bridge, Highway and Transportation District to achieve its mission. *www.parksconservancy.org*

The mission of the Golden Gate Bridge, Highway and Transportation District is to provide safe and reliable operation, maintenance, and enhancement of the Golden Gate Bridge and to provide transportation services, as resources allow, for customers within the US Highway 101 Golden Gate Corridor. *www.goldengatebridge.org*

Developed and designed in the United States, printed and bound in Hong Kong